COMPLETE

COW FARMING

<u>PRO GUIDE</u>

How To Raise Healthy Cattle, Managing Livestock, Maximizing Productivity, And Sustainable Farming Practices For Beginners And Experienced Farmers Tips On Dairy Production, Breeding, Nutrition, Health Care, And Profitable Marketing Strategies

VERN WILSON

CHAPTER 1 4

OVERVIEW OF COW FARMING 4

   Why Farm Cows..4

   Farming Cow Types 5

   General Cow Farming Terminology 6

CHAPTER 2 9

   GETTING STARTED 9

CHAPTER 3 12

   COW BREEDS AND SELECTION 12

   Dairy Cow Breeds..12

   Breeds of Beef Cattle 14

   Combined Use Cow Breeds 15

   Cow Selection Considerations...16

CHAPTER 4 19

   HOUSING AND FACILITIES 19

   Introduction 22

CHAPTER 6 26

   HEALTH MANAGEMENT 26

CHAPTER 7 30

   BREEDING AND PRODUCTION...30

CHAPTER 8 34

   THE MILK AND DAIRY PRODUCTION 34

CHAPTER 9 38

   PRODUCTION OF BEEF...38

   Management Techniques for Beef Cattle 38

   Processing of Meat and Slaughtering.......................................40

   Strategies in Marketing and Sales:...42

CHAPTER 10 45

   FINANCIAL MANAGEMENT...45

   Budgeting and Estimating of Costs...45

   Profitability Analysis and Income Sources 46

   Journaling and Budgeting..47

CHAPTER 11 ....**50**

THE SUSTAINABLE FARMING PRACTICES 50

CHAPTER 12 ....**54**

NEXT TRENDS AND INNOVATIONS...54

CONCLUSION 59

Chapter 1
Overview Of Cow Farming

Starting a cow farming operation is a move with a lot of promise for several reasons. The many advantages of cow farming—from dairy production to meat and byproduct use—make it appealing. Anyone stepping into this agricultural field must understand the subtleties of cow farming, including the kinds of cows appropriate for various reasons and the basic language required.

Why Farm Cows

Many times, several strong reasons motivate people to choose to raise cows. A key driver is the consistent need for dairy products, which are essential to the world food sector. Many homes throughout the world depend on milk, cheese, butter, and other dairy derivatives, which indicates the steady demand for dairy goods in the market. Cow producers who want to make money long-term in agriculture will find this need to be a reliable source of income.

Through the production of meat, cow farming also presents chances for diversification. Since beef is a frequently consumed protein source, farmers wishing to supply the meat market may find great success raising cattle. Furthermore, cows give the farming operation important byproducts like dung for organic fertilizer and hides for leather manufacture.

Farming Cow Types

Knowing the several kinds of cows and how well they work for particular uses is essential to anyone starting a cow farm. Breeds with a high milk output are the main focus of dairy farming. For instance, dairy farmers like Holstein cows because of their well-known high milk outputs. Breeds are also prized for their milk quality and butterfat content—two crucial factors in the production of dairy products—are Jerseys and Guernseys.

But cattle husbandry concentrates on breeds valued for their ability to provide meat. Popular cow breeds Angus and Hereford are chosen for beef production operations because of their marbling and flavor qualities.

The varied requirements of the meat market are met by the meat yield and growth traits of Simmental and Charolaise cattle.

Beyond raising dairy and beef, dual-purpose breeds like Brown Swiss and Shorthorns give farmers flexibility in their farming pursuits by balancing the production of milk and meat. Farmers may decide wisely depending on their farming goals and market demands by knowing the unique features and qualities of each cow breed.

General Cow Farming Terminology

It takes an understanding of basic jargon essential to the business to navigate the world of cow farming. Among important terms are:

I. Calf: Usually less than a year old, a young cattle.

2.Heifer: A young, uncalved female cow.

3. Bull: An older, male cow kept for breeding.

4. A mature female cow has given birth and can produce milk.

5. A male steer, castrated, is reared for beef.

6. Let cows graze on grassland or pasture.

7. Cow milking parlor: Building or space used for this purpose.

Eight. In a feedlot, cattle are fattened for meat production in a contained space.

Nine. Matting bulls and cows for reproduction is known as breeding.

Ten. To maximize grassland use, cows are rotated through several grazing zones.

Application of best practices in animal care, breeding, and management and efficient communication within the cow farming community depends on an understanding of these words. Using language well guarantees maximum output in cow farming endeavors and improves operational efficiency.

Finally, for farmers looking for successful and sustainable agricultural endeavors, cow farming presents a plethora of options. Cow farming offers opportunities for economic expansion and agricultural innovation in everything from dairy production to meat and byproduct use. Success in this exciting and satisfying field is firmly based on knowledge of the reasons behind choosing cow farming, the kinds of cows appropriate for various uses, and the basic jargon.

Chapter 2
Getting Started

Success in starting a cow farm depends on several important factors. One of the first stages of this trip is careful preparation. This includes defining your objectives, knowing the subtleties of cow farming, and writing a strong business strategy. Making strategic decisions about land and infrastructure needs, legal and regulatory issues, financial planning, and marketing plans are all part of designing a cow farm.

The success of a cow farm is mostly dependent on land and infrastructure. Your selection of property should be grazing-friendly and have access to supplies of clean water. Your operation will determine how much land you need; bigger farms need more area for infrastructural construction and grazing. Infrastructure-wise, you will need to think about building fences, shelters or barns, systems for watering and feeding, and equipment and feed storage. Maximizing output and guaranteeing the health of your cattle depend on effective infrastructure design.

When beginning a cow farm, legal and regulatory issues are crucial. To guarantee adherence and stay out of possible legal hot water, become familiar with the local zoning laws, environmental rules, and agricultural policies. Operating a cattle farm may require licenses or permits, particularly if you intend to sell meat or dairy products commercially. Furthermore, morally and sustainably farming requires knowledge of animal welfare norms and best practices.

A further essential component of starting a cow farm is financial planning. This covers approximating possible revenue streams, continuing costs, and beginning costs. Purchase or lease of land, infrastructure development, cattle, feed, and equipment purchases, and, if necessary, personnel hire may all be part of the startup expenditures. Feed, veterinary care, utilities, upkeep, and labor are usually ongoing costs. To make sure your cow farm can survive financially, you need to develop a reasonable budget and financial estimates.

Promotion of your cow farm and contact with prospective clients need marketing plans.

This could entail coming up with a brand identity, putting together a marketing strategy, and using social media, websites, neighborhood markets, and agricultural events among other marketing channels. Emphasizing the caliber of your offerings, ecologically friendly agricultural methods, and animal welfare regulations might draw in clients who respect moral and ecological items.

Establishing a cow farm involves careful preparation that covers aspects like the need for land and infrastructure, legal and regulatory compliance, financial planning, and marketing programs. Strategically addressing these important areas can lay a strong basis for a profitable and long-lasting cow-farming enterprise.

Chapter 3
Cow Breeds And Selection

Farmers have many choices when it comes to cow breeds and selection depending on their particular objectives and their surroundings. Successful cattle ranching requires knowledge of the several cow breeds, their traits, and selection considerations. Let us get further into these ideas.

Dairy Cow Breeds

Since dairy cow breeds are mostly raised for their milk output, dairy farming enterprises find them to be perfect. Among the most often used dairy cow breeds are Brown Swiss, Ayrshire, Guernsey, Holstein, and Jersey.

1. Holstein: The most often chosen breed for dairy farming worldwide, Holstein cows are renowned for their high milk production. Their demeanor is calm and their black and white markings make them identifiable.

2. Though smaller than Holsteins, Jersey cows are renowned for their thick, creamy milk with a high butterfat level. Their efficiency in turning grain into milk makes them valuable and climate-adaptable.

3. Guernsey: High protein and butterfat content milk from Guernsey cows is ideal for creating cheese and butter. Additionally well-known is their fawn or golden-red hue.

4. Ayrshire: Hardy and suited to pasture, Ayrshire cows are wonderful. They are renowned for their longevity and fertility and yield milk with a moderate butterfat level.

5. Brown Swiss: The gentle nature and climate adaptation of brown Swiss cows are well-known. They yield milk that is good for making cheese since it is strong in protein and butterfat.

Regarding temperament, milk output, feed efficiency, and environmental adaptability, every breed of dairy cow is different. Breeds of dairy cows are frequently selected by farmers according to their objectives for production, the resources at their disposal, and the demand for particular dairy goods on the market.

Breeds of Beef Cattle

Breeds of beef cows are selected mostly for their meat, and growth rate, carcass quality, and feed efficiency are among the considerations used in their selection. Common beef cow breeds include Limousin, Simmental, Charolais, Hereford, and Angus.

1. Angus: The marbling that Angus cattle are renowned for enhances the flavor and tenderness of their meat. Black in color, they work effectively in systems that are fed either grain or grass.

2. Hereford: The cattle raised here are renowned for their easygoing nature and effective feed-to-meat conversion. They feature a white underbelly, chest, and face on a crimson body.

3. Cattle classified as Charolais have huge frames and coats that are either white or cream.

They are perfect for producing meat because of their great muscle yield and quick growth rate.

4. Simmental: Well renowned for their maternal traits, rapid development rates, and effective feed conversion, Simmental cattle are adaptable. Their coats come in red, black, and white among other hues.

5. Limousin: High feed efficiency and lean meat are hallmarks of Limousin cattle. Their coats are characteristic golden-red, and their carcasses are prized.

The growth traits, meat quality, and system adaptability of various breeds of cattle are all varied.

When choosing a breed of beef cow for their enterprise, farmers take into account things like market demand, land availability, and desired beef qualities.

Combined Use Cow Breeds

Breeds of cows used for both milk and meat production, or dual-purpose cows, combine features of the dairy and beef breeds. Distinguished dual-purpose cow breeds include the Dutch Belted, Shorthorn, and Brown Swiss.

1. As was already indicated, Brown Swiss cows are ideal for dual-purpose farming because of their excellent milk yield and ability to produce meat.

2. Shorthorn: Raised for either milk or meat, shorthorn cattle are renowned for their adaptability. Red, white, or roan in color, they are prized for their placid demeanor.

3. Dutch Belted: A characteristic black or red belt around their belly distinguishes Dutch Belted cattle. These animals are good dual-purpose producers of milk and meat.

Breeds of dual-purpose cows allow farmers to produce both dairy and beef without concentrating on one area. Selecting dual-purpose breeds is up to farmers' tastes, available resources, and market prospects.

Several considerations affect cow selection for a farming business to guarantee maximum profitability and productivity:

I. Production Goals: Whether they be for producing milk, meat, or a combination of both, farmers should specify their production goals. Breeds that support these objectives are more easily chosen as a result.

2. Environment: As various cow breeds are more or less suited to particular locations, take into account the climate, topography, and resources available on the farm.

3. Feed Efficiency: As this directly affects running expenses and total profitability, assess the feed efficiency of various breeds.

4. Market Demand: Think about what your area's dairy, beef, or dual-purpose cattle markets are. Select breeds that correspond with consumer tastes and fashions.

Five. Breeds with a reputation for longevity, fertility, and good health will lower your herd's risk of health problems and extend its lifespan.

When choosing cows for your farm, take into account also things like temperament, ease of calving, maintenance needs, and genetic features linked to disease resistance and productivity.

Successful cow selection in farming operations requires a grasp of the traits of various cow breeds, including dairy, beef, and dual-purpose breeds, as well as taking into account production goals, environment, feed efficiency, market demand, and health issues. Every breed presents different benefits and difficulties, therefore farmers must choose wisely according to their requirements and goals when raising cattle.

Chapter 4
Housing And Facilities

Successful cow ranching depends critically on the design and construction of cow barns. While guaranteeing effective management procedures, the comfort and well-being of the cows should be given priority in the barn's architecture.

An excellently planned barn offers protection from the weather, encourages adequate ventilation, makes feeding and watering simple, and encourages appropriate waste management.

A cow barn's design must take several things into account. About their size, habit, and comfort needs, the arrangement should provide enough room for each cow. Cows ought to be able to walk about freely without being crowded, lie down, and rise. For added stress reduction and health promotion, the barn should include distinct sections for feeding, resting, and calving.

Durable materials should be used to build the cow barn so that it can resist daily abuse and offer insulation from cold. Injury prevention and hygienic promotion depend on proper flooring. While cozy resting places with enough bedding encourage cow comfort and health, non-slip flooring in feeding and walking areas lowers the chance of mishaps.

The system of watering and feeding cows is very important in cow management. Cows are guaranteed to have a balanced diet based on their requirements via effective feeding systems. This entails giving fresh water access at all times and supplying suitable feed rations according to the stage of production of each cow. Automatic feeding systems guarantee constant access to food all day long and can help simplify the feeding procedure.

A system for watering cows should be made to provide them with fresh, clean water free from contamination. Important factors to encourage cows to drink enough water—which is necessary for their health and milk output—are adequate water pressure and the availability of water sources.

The cow barn needs to be kept comfortable and healthy by temperature and ventilation regulations. Air quality is improved and respiratory problems are reduced when moisture, smells, and airborne pollutants are removed via proper ventilation. For best airflow, mechanical ventilation systems may be added to natural ventilation from windows, vents, and ridge openings.

It takes blowers, heaters, and insulation to control indoor temperatures and keep cows from becoming too hot or too cold. Cows can be kept cool in hot weather by fans or misters, and warm in colder months by insulation and heating systems.

All things considered, a well-planned and built cow barn with effective watering and feeding systems, enough ventilation, and temperature regulation improves the health, comfort, and output of cows in an agricultural business. By reducing environmental effects and making the best use of available resources, it also promotes ethical and sustainable farming methods.

Introduction

Cow farming operations cannot be successful unless one understands the cow's diet. Like all animals, cows need a balanced diet to stay healthy, thrive, and support reproductive processes.

This knowledge includes several things, such as feeding schedules, different kinds of feed and supplements, and general feeding management techniques.

Being ruminant animals, cows can effectively break down fibrous plant materials thanks to their sophisticated digestive systems. Roughage—grass, hay, and silage—makes up most of their diet and supplies vital nutrients like proteins, carbs, vitamins, and minerals. Knowing the makeup of these feeds and how they support general health and productivity is essential to comprehending the nutritional requirements of cows.

Meeting cows' nutritional needs depends critically on the kinds of feed and additives used. They eat mostly forage, which includes legumes and pasture grass.

It supplies fiber, which is necessary for rumen health fermentation and nutrient
absorption. Concentrates provide concentrated supplies of energy and protein, therefore supplementing the diet. Examples of concentrates are grains and feeds high in protein.

Cows are guaranteed enough energy, protein, vitamins, and minerals by balancing these elements for the best performance.

Further improving nutritional balance are supplements. Among these are mineral supplements such as salt blocks, which supply trace, phosphorus, and calcium—all vital minerals for the growth of bones, the operation of muscles, and general metabolism. Particularly in regions where specific vitamins are lacking in the forage, vitamin supplements could also be required.

Critical components of cow nutrition are the feeding plan and management. Setting up a regular feeding plan supports the health of the rumen and the effectiveness of the digestion.

Because cows do best when they are routinely fed, feeding times should be set up and spaced over the day.

Cows are also guaranteed fresh, nutrient-dense feed free of pollutants or spoiling by management of feed quality and availability.

In larger herds, in particular, feeding management also includes factors like group vs individual feeding. Though it makes management easier, group feeding needs close observation to guarantee that every cow gets the nutrients it needs. Though more work and resources are needed, individual feeding gives exact control over each cow's diet.

Regular evaluations of body condition, milk output, and general health are part of monitoring cow nutrition. These evaluations, seasonal variations, or particular nutritional needs throughout lactation, gestation, or growth periods may require adjustments to feed composition or supplements.

All things considered, comprehending cow nutrition calls for a comprehensive approach that takes into account feed quality, supplements, feeding schedules, and management techniques catered to specific cow requirements and farm circumstances. Based on productive and healthy cows, good nutrition is necessary for lucrative and sustained cow farming operations.

Chapter 6
Health Management

Aspects of health management in cow farming include vaccination and deworming schedules implementation, common cow diseases management, and preventative healthcare measures. These components are essential to keeping cattle herds productive and well.

The cornerstone of any profitable cow farming operation is preventive healthcare procedures. This includes keeping the herd clean and hygienic, as well as routinely checking on its health and nutrition. By early detection of any possible abnormalities, regular health exams by licensed veterinarians enable prompt management and the avoidance of more serious health issues. In addition, farmers have to make sure their cows have access to clean water and appropriate shelter from bad weather.

Since common cow diseases can seriously affect the health and production of the herd, farmers are always concerned about them.

Early identification and treatment of many illnesses depend on a knowledge of their signs. Mastitis, foot rot, respiratory infections, and reproductive problems are a few typical cow illnesses. Farmers must be aware of the warning indications of these illnesses and have procedures in place for their control.

Veterinary care, drugs, and appropriate management techniques are combined in the treatment of common cow diseases. The particular illness and its severity may determine the usage of antibiotics, anti-inflammatory medications, and supportive therapy. Working closely with veterinarians, farmers may create efficient treatment programs and follow-up care that guarantee the health and recovery of afflicted cows.

Part of preventative healthcare in cow farming is vaccinations and deworming. Cows are better

protected against   infectious
diseases including clostridial   infections,   infectious
bovine rhinotracheitis (IBR), and bovine viral diarrhea
(BVD) by vaccinations.

Veterinary advice should be sought for when choosing
and administering vaccines, and farmers should adhere
to suggested vaccination regimens determined by the
incidence of diseases in their area.

Controlling internal parasites that can harm cow
productivity and health requires deworming. Frequent
deworming regimens—usually every two to three
months—help ward against parasite infestations and
lower   the   chance   of   associated   health
problems including diarrhea,   weight   loss,   and
decreased milk production.

To   reduce   the   emergence   of   parasite
resistance, farmers should use and alternate effective
deworming drugs.

In general, good health management techniques—
preventive measures, illness treatment, vaccinations,

and deworming—are necessary to guarantee the welfare, health, and output of cows on a farm.

The performance and profitability of their herd can be maximized while upholding high standards of animal welfare by farmers who give cow health priority and put in place thorough healthcare procedures.

Chapter 7

Breeding And Production

A healthy herd and good breeding depend heavily on an understanding of cow reproduction cycles.

Like many mammals, cows have discrete reproductive stages that are essential to their mating habits. Hormonal changes affecting estrus (heat) and ovulation are what mostly regulate the cow's reproductive cycle.

Known by most as the heat cycle, the estrous cycle is the first step in comprehending cow reproduction cycles. Though it can differ from cow to cow, this cycle usually lasts about 21 days. The cow shows physical and behavioral changes at this time that suggest she is ready to mate. More vocalization, mounting of other cows or objects, restlessness, and obvious mucus flow from the vulva are symptoms of estrus.

Proestrus, estrus, metestrus, and diestrus are the four primary phases of the estrous cycle. The last stage before estrus starts is called proestrus.

Hormonal changes start here.

When a cow is most fertile and eager to mate, it occurs during estrus, the height of her sexual reactivity. Before diestrus, when the cow's reproductive system gets ready for a possible pregnancy, comes metestrus.

Optimizing cow reproductive performance depends critically on breeding strategies and practices.

In commercial operations particularly, artificial insemination (AI) is a widely used technique for cow breeding.

AI is gathering a bull's semen and artificially inseminating a cow at the appropriate estrous cycle point. Genetic selection and regulated breeding made possible by this method raise the quality and production of herds.

Natural mating is another method of breeding in which a bull is let to mate with a cow during her estrus period.

More often used in smaller operations or when precise genetic characteristics are sought from a certain bull is this approach.

Part of cow reproduction cycles are pregnancy care and calving management. Once a cow is successfully bred, the health and welfare of the developing calf as well as the cow must be guaranteed by appropriate pregnancy care. This covers routine veterinary exams, a suitable diet catered to the cow's pregnancy stage, and troubleshooting.

Calving management is getting the cow ready for and supporting her during her birth. This covers making the calving area hygienic and secure, offering help as needed, and making sure the newborn calf is given the right care right away after birth.

Calving management done correctly lowers the possibility of problems and encourages normal calf growth.

All things considered, the foundation of a successful and long-lasting cattle breeding program is knowledge of cow reproduction cycles, the use of efficient breeding methods, and the implementation of appropriate pregnancy care and calving management. Through process optimization, farmers can raise the genetics, productivity, and general profitability of their herds.

Chapter 8
The Milk And Dairy Production

Dairy production and milking include a wide range of operations and procedures that are necessary to guarantee a consistent and high-quality supply of milk and dairy products. This thorough book will go into many facets of milking, dairy production, equipment, methods, handling, storage, processing of dairy products, and marketing plans.

Methods and Equipment for Milking: The basis of effective and hygienic milk production is formed by methods and equipment for milking. To speed up the milking process, modern dairy farms use cutting-edge milking technology like milking machines, automated teat cleaners, and milk meters. Since pulsation systems in milking machines now resemble those in hand milking, they guarantee gentle and thorough milk extraction while preserving the health of the udder.

The highest possible milk yield and quality depend on using correct milking methods.

To reduce the possibility of contamination and guarantee cow satisfaction, farmers receive training in procedures including pre-milking udder preparation, appropriate milking unit attachment, and post-milking teat disinfection. Additionally necessary to avoid breakdowns and preserve maximum milking efficiency are routine maintenance and calibration of the milking equipment.

Milk Storage and Handling Techniques: To protect the safety and quality of milk, after milking, correct storage and handling techniques are essential. Milk storage techniques used by dairy farms include bulk milk tanks with cooling systems that quickly lower milk temperature and stop bacterial growth. Milk freshness is maintained and bacterial contamination is avoided by proper ventilation and cleaning of storage facilities.

A lot of the time, milk is moved from farms to dairy processing facilities in specially designed tanker trucks that keep the temperature under control. When milk gets to processing plants, it is put through a lot of testing for quality factors including lipid content, protein levels, and bacterial counts before being turned into different dairy products.

Processing and Marketing of Dairy Products: Processing dairy products is the process of converting raw milk into a variety of goods, including cheese, yogurt, butter, and powdered milk.

The intended product determines the processing methods; cheese production includes pasteurization, homogenization, fermentation, and aging. Extended shelf life and worldwide distribution of dairy products are made possible by cutting-edge technology including aseptic packaging and ultra-high temperature (UHT) processing.

Promoting dairy products and extending market reach are made possible in large part by marketing plans. In a cutthroat industry, dairy companies use branding, advertising, product diversification, and strategic alliances to attract customers and set themselves apart from their competitors. Within the dairy sector, consumer trends include the need for organic, lactose-free, and plant-based dairy substitutes affect product development and marketing plans.

To sum up, milking and dairy production include a sophisticated network of tools, procedures, storage conditions, processing procedures, and marketing plans meant to provide consumers all over the world with safe, superior dairy products. The dairy sector is succeeding and expanding mostly because of ongoing innovation, quality standards compliance, and sustainable practices.

Chapter 9
Production Of Beef

A complicated and multidimensional sector, beef production includes everything from cow management to slaughtering, meat processing, and marketing plans. Delivering premium beef products to consumers while guaranteeing producers' profitability and sustainability depends on each component. Let us go into great depth on the fundamental ideas of producing beef.

Management Techniques for Beef Cattle

Production of beef depends critically on the management techniques used for cattle. All of the care, feeding, breeding, and health management of cattle is included. Assuring enough nutrition for the best possible growth and development is one of the main factors in managing beef cattle. This includes feeding calves, growing cattle, and breeding stock a balanced diet that satisfies their various nutritional needs. In beef cattle management, it is standard procedure to graze on pastureland and supplement with hay, grains, and feeds high in protein.

In managing beef cattle, breeding strategies are also rather important. Breeding stock is generally chosen by producers according to desired characteristics including growth rate, meat quality, disease resistance, and reproductive performance.

The objectives and available resources of the operation will determine which breeding techniques—from natural mating to artificial insemination (AI) and embryo transfer—are used.

A further important component of managing beef cattle is health management. This includes routine veterinarian care, parasite control, immunization programs for disease prevention, and appropriate herd management techniques to reduce stress and guarantee general health. Tracking performance indicators, genetic information, and health histories also requires data management and herd records.

All things considered, efficient methods of managing beef cattle seek to maximize producer income, reduce risks, and maximize output, as well as animal welfare and sustainability.

Processing of Meat and Slaughtering

Crucial phases in beef production that turn live animals into edible meat products are slaughtering and meat processing. Usually, the procedure starts with moving cattle to a processing plant where they are slaughtered humanely by industry best practices and regulations. The animals are handled and stunning properly to minimize stress and suffering.

Following slaughter, qualified experts examine corpses for quality and safety. Evaluations of aspects including fat content, marbling, muscular growth, and general health are part of this. Systems for classifying meat according to quality characteristics and market value include USDA beef categories (Prime, Choice, Select, etc.).

Beef products are prepared, portioned, packaged, and distributed to merchants, food service outlets, and consumers through a sequence of procedures known as sausage processing. This includes removing extra fat, chopping into different cuts (e.g., ground beef, steaks, roasts), maturing to create taste, packaging (cryovac, vacuum sealing, etc.), and labeling for traceability and product identification.

Modern meat processing plants use cutting-edge equipment and food safety protocols to guarantee the quality, shelf life, and hygienic requirements of their output. This includes microbial testing, cold chain management, HACCP (Hazard Analysis and Critical Control Points) procedures, and regulatory compliance.

Meat processing includes not just fresh beef products but also value-added items like sausages, burgers, marinated pieces, and prepared dinners. Consumer tastes for convenience, variety of flavors, and culinary adaptability are met by these items.

Strategies in Marketing and Sales:

A vital part of beef production, marketing, and sales plans entails introducing, distributing, and selling beef products to specific markets. Knowledge of consumer preferences, market trends, and competition dynamics is the first step toward effective marketing. To find prospects, evaluate demand drivers, and create strategic marketing plans, producers and other industry stakeholders frequently carry out market research.

A major component of beef marketing is product differentiation and branding. Using quality characteristics, certifications (such as organic, and grass-fed), sustainability measures, and animal welfare requirements, one can develop value offers that appeal to customers. Advertisement campaigns, social media presence, product labeling, and joint ventures with merchants and food service operators are all possible components of branding activities.

Reaching various client groups and extending market reach are made possible in large part by distribution networks.

Along with internet channels and direct-to-consumer sales strategies, this includes conventional channels including supermarkets, butcher shops, and restaurants. Effective logistics, inventory control, and market penetration are facilitated by strategic alliances with wholesalers, distributors, and other supply chain participants.

Pricing plans, promotions, discounts, and incentives are all part of sales tactics; they are intended to increase profitability, increase sales volume, and increase demand. To involve customers and encourage repeat purchases, this could include seasonal incentives, bundling possibilities, loyalty programs, and focused marketing campaigns.

Moreover, efficient marketing and sales plans in the beef sector depend on consumer involvement and education.

Giving consumers knowledge of beef cuts, preparation methods, health advantages, and recipe ideas improves their confidence in their culinary abilities and general contentment with beef goods.

 to promote expansion and profitability in a cutthroat industry, effective marketing and sales plans in the beef industry concentrate on value creation, market response, consumer involvement, and strategic alliances.

Chapter 10
Financial Management

Fundamental components of personal, corporate, and organizational financial management are cost estimation and budgeting. While budgeting is allocating resources to fulfill certain expenses within a given timeline, cost estimating is projecting the costs related to a certain project, activity, or period. Reaching financial goals, efficiently managing resources, and guaranteeing financial stability all depend on accurate cost estimation and planning.

Finding all of the costs associated with a project or activity is the first step in a cost estimate. This covers overhead charges such as utilities, rent, and administrative costs as well as direct costs like supplies, labor, and equipment. Precise cost estimation calls for in-depth investigation, historical data analysis, and taking into account several variables that could affect costs, such as inflation, market trends, and regulatory changes.

Budgeting comes next once expenses are estimated. A budget is a plan of financial allocation of resources to meet projected costs and accomplish financial goals. Usually, it contains a schedule for financial operations together with estimates of income and expenses. Budgeting facilitates the setting of priorities for expenditure, monitoring of financial results, and well-informed allocation of resources.

Profitability Analysis and Income Sources

Important elements of financial management are knowing the sources of money and carrying out profitability analysis. Income sources are the several revenue sources that support the financial inflows of a person or organization. These might include investments, grants, loans, sales revenue, and other funding sources. It is usually advised to diversify income sources to lessen reliance on one and increase financial stability.

To ascertain a business's or activity's profitability, financial performance is evaluated. Revenue, costs, profit margins, ROI, and other financial measures are among the things this study takes into account. It makes judgments based on data to increase profitability, evaluates the efficacy of company plans, and points up areas of strength and weakness.

It takes precise financial information, financial accounts, and performance indicators to analyze income sources and profitability. Measurement of performance and variation identification also entails comparing actual outcomes with expected or budgeted data. Revenue generating, cost-effectiveness, pricing tactics, and general financial health are all shown by this examination.

Journaling and Budgeting

Essential financial management techniques, record-keeping, and financial planning support compliance, strategic decision-making, and organizational effectiveness.

Accurate and well-organized financial records covering revenue, expenses, assets, obligations, and transactions are maintained by record keeping. It guarantees responsibility, openness, and observance of accounting rules and reporting requirements.

Financial reporting, audits, and analysis are all made easier by good recordkeeping. It offers a record of financial transactions, patterns, and performance measures for use in strategic planning and decision-making. The use of cloud-based systems and accounting software among other modern technology has simplified record-keeping procedures, enabling real-time access to financial data and improved data security.

Developing a financial plan is laying out a road map for reaching financial objectives. Financial goals must be established, plans must be created to reach them, and resources must be allocated wisely. Budgeting, investing, risk management, retirement, and estate planning are just a few of the many facets of financial planning. It builds a thorough financial plan suited to the requirements of the individual or the business by taking into account elements like income, expenses, savings, investments, taxes, and insurance.

Financial management, thus, includes financial planning, record keeping, income sources, profitability analysis, and cost estimation and budgeting. These ideas are related and necessary for the success, expansion, and financial stability of people, companies, and organizations. Financial performance must be continuously monitored and evaluated, strategic planning must be done, and attention to detail must be maintained.

Chapter 11
The Sustainable Farming Practices

A variety of approaches aiming at enhancing biodiversity, lowering environmental effects, and guaranteeing the long-term sustainability of agricultural systems are included in sustainable farming methods.

In the context of cow farming, reducing the ecological impact of livestock activities is mostly dependent on environmental protection.

Using organic and natural agricultural techniques, recycling, and waste management are just a few of the factors that go into putting sustainable practices into cow farming.

In cow production, environmental conservation is a complex field with several approaches to reduce adverse effects on ecosystems.

Land management is one important factor, as is rotational grazing methods that stop soil erosion and let pasturelands regrow.

Farmers may keep healthy grasslands, increase soil fertility, and use fewer chemicals by rotating grazing areas.

Water conservation is yet another essential component of environmentally friendly cattle raising.

Water wastage is decreased and this valuable resource is guaranteed to be available for crops and livestock by efficient use of water, such as drip irrigation systems and rainwater gathering.

By filtering runoff and halting soil erosion, techniques like establishing riparian buffers along water bodies also help preserve the quality of the water.

Sustainable cow farming methods depend heavily on biodiversity conservation. On farms, natural areas like wetlands and woods that are preserved benefit a variety of plant and animal species.

Including agroforestry systems—trees and shrubs mixed into grazing areas—offers other advantages including wildlife habitat, carbon sequestration, and cattle shade.

Basic elements of sustainable cow ranching include recycling and waste management. Manure and other agricultural wastes handled effectively lower pollution hazards and improve soil health.

Composting is one of the methods that converts organic waste into soil amendments high in nutrients, therefore finishing the nutrient cycle and reducing the demand for synthetic fertilizers.

Fundamental to sustainable cow farming techniques are organic and natural agricultural techniques.

By outlawing the use of antibiotics, synthetic pesticides, and genetically modified organisms (GMOs), organic farming promotes biodiversity and soil health.

On farms, natural farming methods include using beneficial insects to control pests and adding cover crops to strengthen soil structure and improve ecological balance.

Using sustainable farming methods in cow production calls for a comprehensive strategy that takes social, economic, and environmental aspects into account. To demonstrate their dedication to ethical land management, farmers might join in sustainable agricultural projects or take up certification schemes like USDA Organic. Cow farmers help to build a more robust and sustainable agricultural system by giving environmental conservation, waste management, and the adoption of organic and natural farming techniques priority.

Chapter 12

Next Trends And Innovations

The management and operation of cow farms have been revolutionized by the tremendous technological breakthroughs of recent years. In data collecting and processing, for example, technology has had a major influence. Sensors and monitoring equipment on contemporary farms monitor several facets of cow activity and health. Wearable gadgets, like GPS trackers and RFID tags, enable farmers, for instance, to track individual cows, track their movements, and collect information on their activity levels. One can use this information to find trends, spot health problems early on, and improve breeding and feeding procedures.

Automated milking systems represent yet another technological advancement in cow husbandry. Cows can be milked by these systems—also referred to as robotic milking—without human assistance. The cows freely access the milking station where robotic arms attach and remove milking equipment, check the quality of the milk, and log information on the amount of milk produced by each cow.

Because they offer consistent milking procedures, automated milking systems not only save labor expenses but also raise milk yield and quality.

Another technique that is becoming more popular in cow farming is precision farming. This method uses sensors, drones, and GPS mapping to accurately control inputs to farms including fertilizers, water, and feed. Precision farming methods apply to cow farming to improve grazing patterns, track pasture health, and more effectively manage herd movements. Precision farming raises farm productivity and sustainability by reducing waste and optimizing resource use.

Additionally influencing the direction of cow farming are new developments in livestock management. Among these trends is the combination of farm management software with digital platforms. Farmer tools for herd management, health monitoring, financial analysis, and decision-making assistance are provided by these platforms. Better farm performance and profitability result from farmers making more educated and data-driven decisions made possible by digital platforms, which centralize data and offer real-time insight.

In cow farming, too, genomic technologies are becoming increasingly important. Through improvements in genetic testing and breeding methods, farmers can now choose for desired characteristics including feed efficiency, disease resistance, and milk production. Breeding choices can be made by farmers that enhance herd genetics and total farm profitability by using genomic information.

Apart from technical developments, the cow farming sector is confronted with several prospects and problems. The expanding market for sustainable and organic dairy products presents one opportunity. Customers' growing concerns about the quality of food, the treatment of animals, and the environment are driving demand for dairy products from farms that give sustainability and moral behavior priority.

Cow farmers have a chance with this trend to set themselves apart from the competition and enter high-end market niches.

Conversely, market volatility, animal welfare laws, and environmental sustainability are other issues that the cow farming sector must deal with. Concerns about environmental sustainability include things like livestock emissions of greenhouse gases, manure runoff contaminating water, and deforestation for pasture expansion. Pressure to adopt sustainable methods, lessen their environmental impact, and lessen the effects of climate change is mounting on cow farmers.

Regulations about animal welfare provide still another obstacle for the cow farming sector. As public awareness of animal welfare issues grows, there is increasing scrutiny and regulation of farming practices related to cow health, housing conditions, and treatment. Farmers need to stay compliant with evolving regulations and invest in animal welfare measures to maintain consumer trust and market access.

Market volatility is a perennial challenge for cow farmers, with fluctuating prices for milk and dairy products influenced by factors such as supply and demand dynamics, global economic conditions, and trade policies. Farmers must navigate market uncertainties, manage production costs, and explore diversification strategies to mitigate risks and maintain financial stability.

Technology is driving significant innovations in cow farming, from data-driven management practices to automated milking systems and precision farming techniques. These advancements offer opportunities for improved productivity, sustainability, and profitability in the industry. However, challenges such as environmental sustainability, animal welfare regulations, and market volatility require proactive management and strategic planning to ensure the long-term success of cow farming operations.

Conclusion

This comprehensive guide on cow farming covers every aspect, from the basics of why one should choose cow farming to advanced topics like future trends and innovations in the industry. It provides a roadmap for aspiring and experienced farmers alike, starting with understanding cow breeds and selection, planning and setting up the farm, managing nutrition and health, to optimizing production for dairy or beef.

The book delves into the intricacies of housing and facilities, emphasizing the importance of a well-designed cow barn and efficient feeding systems. It also delves into the nuances of cow nutrition, covering various feed types, supplements, and feeding schedules for optimal health and productivity.

Health management is another crucial aspect discussed comprehensively, from preventive healthcare practices to dealing with common diseases and maintaining vaccination schedules. Reproduction and breeding techniques are explored in detail, along with guidance on calving management and dairy production processes.

Financial aspects are not overlooked, with detailed sections on cost estimation, budgeting, income sources, and profitability analysis. The book also highlights sustainable farming practices, including environmental conservation, waste management, and organic farming methods.

The discussion extends to future trends and innovations in cow farming, incorporating insights into technology adoption, emerging trends in livestock management, and the opportunities and challenges facing the industry. Overall, this book serves as a valuable resource for anyone involved or interested in the field of cow farming, offering a comprehensive and practical guide to success in this dynamic industry.